STECK-VAUGHN
ACHIEVE
New Jersey
Mathematics
3

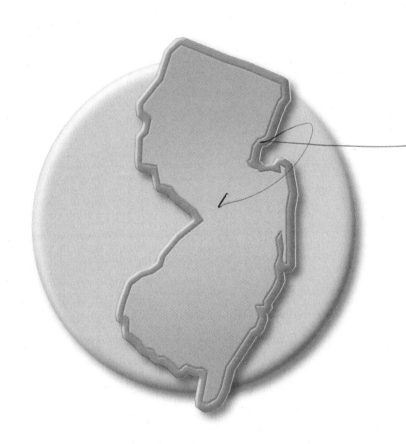

Harcourt Achieve

Rigby • Saxon • Steck-Vaughn

www.HarcourtAchieve.com
1.800.531.5015

ISBN 1-4190-1487-0

1 2 3 4 5 6 7 8 9 10 082 12 11 10 09 08 07 06 05

Achieve New Jersey
Contents

Standards for New Jersey Mathematics

Numbers and Numerical Operations   You will be expected to —
- show that you understand the meanings and uses of numbers and place value.
- decide if answers to problems are correct.
- estimate the answers to problems when exact answers are not needed.
- show that you understand arithmetic (how to add, subtract, multiply, and divide).
- use numbers to solve real-world problems.

Geometry and Measurement   You will be expected to —
- select and use units of measurement to solve real-life problems.
- find the perimeter of a geometric shape by measuring its sides.
- find the area in square units of a rectangle drawn on a grid.
- tell about and classify plane figures and space figures.
- understand and recognize figures with the same shapes or sizes and figures with lines of symmetry.
- recognize and make flips, turns, and slides of figures.
- find and name points on coordinate grids.

Patterns and Algebra   You will be expected to —
- find, tell about, and continue patterns.
- use models, such as tables, to represent functions.
- write and solve open number sentences.
- recognize and tell about change using graphs.
- use letters to represent numbers that are not known.
- understand and use symbols ($<$, $>$, and $=$) to order and compare numbers.

Data Analysis, Probability, and Discrete Mathematics   You will be expected to —
- sort, classify, and count objects based on ways the objects are alike or different.
- collect and organize data.
- ask and answer questions about data in tables and graphs.
- follow and give directions.
- show you understand vertex-edge graphs and paths in the graphs.
- find and explain the probability of an event and classify it as *impossible, least likely, equally likely, most likely,* or *certain.*

To the Student: About Achieve New Jersey

This book will help you prepare for the Grade 3 NJ ASK Mathematics test.

The first part of the book has six lessons that review mathematics skills and let you practice different kinds of questions you will see on the real test. The six lessons also give you Tips for answering each practice question.

Each lesson covers a different topic or area.

Lesson 1: *Problem-Solving Strategies* provides instructional material and steps to follow when answering questions. It introduces a Four-Step Method for Solving Problems and Nine Problem-Solving Strategies that will strengthen your problem-solving skills.

The remaining five lessons each address a different content cluster. Each lesson consists of instruction with a How to Do It section that gives steps to follow to solve the problem, an On Your Own problem, and a Practice section.

Lesson 2: *Numbers and Numerical Operations* includes making suitable approximations, estimating, understanding numbers, and applying numbers in real-life situations.

Lesson 3: *Geometry* focuses on identifying spatial relationships and applying the principles of geometry, symmetry, congruence, similarity, geometric transformations, and coordinate geometry.

Lesson 4: *Measurement* covers measures of length, capacity, weight, area, perimeter, time, temperature, and volume.

Lesson 5: *Patterns and Algebra* addresses working with patterns, using inductive reasoning, and utilizing algebraic processes and concepts.

Lesson 6: *Data Analysis, Probability, and Discrete Mathematics* explains determining using probabilities; collecting, organizing, and analyzing data; applying the methods and concepts of discrete mathematics; and using patterns and processes to analyze everyday experiences.

The second part of the book contains a practice test that is similar to the NJ ASK Mathematics test. Taking this practice test will help you know what the actual test is like.

The NJ ASK Mathematics test includes questions about numbers and numerical operations, geometry, measurement, patterns, algebra, data analysis, probability, and discrete mathematics. It will ask you to answer questions, solve problems, and use the mathematics skills you have learned. Test questions will help measure how well you understand the skills outlined in the New Jersey Core Curriculum Content Standards for Mathematics.

Kinds of Questions

Multiple-Choice Questions

- After each multiple-choice question, there are four answer choices.
- You will fill in the circle next to your answer choice.

Open-Ended Questions

- These questions do not have answer choices. You need to write out your own answer.
- You may be asked to write a number sentence, give a short written answer, solve a problem, draw a diagram, or make a chart. You may be asked to explain your answer in your own words or to show your work.
- There can be more than one correct answer to some problems. Answer the questions the way you think is best.
- Show all your work as well as your final answer. You may get some points for answering part of a question.

Lesson 1

NJ ASK Modeled Instruction
Problem-Solving Strategies

It is important to know how to think about and solve mathematical problems. The Four-Step Method shown below gives simple steps for you to follow. The nine strategies will help you decide on the best way to find the correct answer.

Follow the **Four-Step Method for Solving Problems**:

Four-Step Method for Solving Problems	
1. **Decide**	*Decide what you need to do.*
2. **Choose**	*Choose the best strategy to use.*
3. **Solve**	*Find the answer to the problem.*
4. **Check**	*Check your answer.*

Choose one of the **Nine Problem-Solving Strategies** to find the correct answer:

Nine Problem-Solving Strategies

1. **Organize the Information**
   A. Draw a Picture
   B. Make a Chart, Graph, or List
   C. Find a Pattern
   D. Sort the Data

2. **Compute/Use Manipulatives**

3. **Estimate**

4. **Make a Simpler Problem**

5. **Write a Number Sentence**

6. **Use a Formula**

7. **Use a Definition or Rule**

8. **Work Backward**

9. **Use Logical Thinking**

1. Organize the Information

A. DRAW A PICTURE

You can draw a picture to solve a problem. A picture will help you see the problem more clearly.

SAMPLE PROBLEM

Cindy wants to jump off the high diving board at the swimming pool. First she climbs 6 steps up the ladder. Then she gets scared and goes down 3 steps. Cindy decides to be brave and climbs up 7 steps to the top of the ladder. What number belongs on the top step of the ladder?

How to Do It

Draw a picture of a ladder and label the steps. Then count the number of steps Cindy climbed.

The top step is number 10.

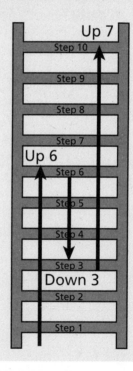

On Your Own

A dog chases a cat up a tree. The cat climbs up to the 9th branch. The dog stops barking and goes away. The cat climbs down 5 branches. Then the dog runs back to the tree and starts barking again. The cat climbs up 13 branches to the top of the tree. What number belongs at the top branch?

B. MAKE A CHART, GRAPH, OR LIST

Organizing information into charts, graphs, or lists helps you to show numbers, see patterns, and list all the possibilities of a problem. Then you can find the answer more easily.

SAMPLE PROBLEM

The temperature at 3:00 P.M. was 70°F. If the temperature drops 4°F every hour, what will the temperature be at 10:00 P.M.?

How to Do It

Organize the information into a chart. Make a column for time and one for temperature. Write the first time, 3:00 P.M. List each hour up to 10:00 P.M. Then write the beginning temperature. Subtract 4 degrees to find the temperature for each hour.

Time (P.M.)	Temperature (F)
3:00	70°
4:00	70° − 4° = 66°
5:00	66° − 4° = 62°
6:00	62° − 4° = 58°
7:00	58° − 4° = 54°
8:00	54° − 4° = 50°
9:00	50° − 4° = 46°
10:00	46° − 4° = 42°

The temperature at 10:00 P.M. will be 42°F.

On Your Own

The temperature at 5:00 A.M. was 62°F. If the temperature rises 2°F every hour, what will the temperature be at 10:00 A.M.

72°F

C. FIND A PATTERN

Patterns can be used to help you decide what will happen next. You can look for a pattern within a problem to find the answer.

SAMPLE PROBLEM

Look at the shape pattern. If this pattern continues, what shape will be in the 26th position?

How to Do It

Find a pattern. The pattern repeats itself after the 5th shape. In the 5th position, there is a rectangle.

Any multiple of 5 will be a rectangle.

Multiples of 5 are 5, 10, 15, 20, 25, 30 . . .

In the 25th position, you will have a rectangle.

The next shape after the rectangle is a hexagon.

In the 26th position, you will have a hexagon.

On Your Own

Examine the pattern: S, U, B, T, R, A, C, T, S, U, B, T, R, A, C, T . . .

If this pattern continues, what letter will be in the 48th position?

...SUBTRACTSUBTRACTS

UBTRACTSUBTRACT

D. SORT THE DATA

You can sort information in a problem to help you solve it. One way to sort information is to put it into groups.

SAMPLE PROBLEM

How many number words from "one" to "twenty" begin with the letter *t*? 6

How to Do It

First write the number word for each number from 1 to 20. Then sort the number words into two groups: number words that begin with *t* and number words that do not begin with *t*.

	Number Words that Begin with *t*	Number Words that Do Not Begin with *t*
one	two	one
two	three	four
three	ten	five
four	twelve	six
five	thirteen	seven
six	twenty	eight
seven		nine
eight		eleven
nine		fourteen
ten		fifteen
eleven		sixteen
twelve		seventeen
thirteen		eighteen
fourteen		nineteen
fifteen		
sixteen		
seventeen		
eighteen		
nineteen		
twenty		

Count how many number words begin with the letter *t*. There are 6 number words from "one" to "twenty" that begin with the letter *t*.

On Your Own

How many number words from "one" to "twenty" end with the letter *n*? 2

2. Compute/Use Manipulatives

For most problems, you need to add, subtract, multiply, or divide. Sometimes you can use objects to help you find the answer. Remember to check your answer to see if it makes sense.

Find the sum of the place-value models.

4,367

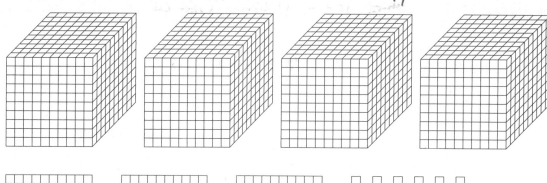

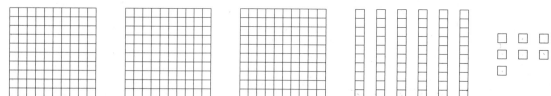

How to Do It

Find the sum of each place-value model.

Thousands	Hundreds	Tens	Ones
4	3	6	7

Find the total sum:

$$
\begin{array}{r}
4,000 \\
300 \\
60 \\
+\quad 7 \\
\hline
\end{array}
$$

The sum of the place-value models is: 4,367

On Your Own

If A = 1, B = 2, C = 3, and so on, find the sum of the fifth word in the third sentence below.

The Macaw is a large parrot that comes from Central and South America. It is about 2 feet long and is very noisy. It has brilliantly colored feathers.

82

3. Estimate

Estimation is used to solve a problem when an exact answer is not needed. You can round large numbers to help you find an answer.

SAMPLE PROBLEM

The third-grade students sold 6,216 candy bars, and the fourth-grade students sold 4,172 candy bars. About how many more candy bars did the third-grade students sell than the fourth-grade students sold? The answer is between what two numbers?

 Ⓐ 500 and 1,500   Ⓒ 2,500 and 3,500

 Ⓑ 1,500 and 2,500   Ⓓ 3,500 and 4,500

How to Do It

You can round both numbers and estimate the difference.

Round each number to the nearest thousand.

6,216 rounds to 6,000

4,172 rounds to 4,000

Find the difference:
$$\begin{array}{r} 6,000 \\ -\ 4,000 \\ \hline 2,000 \end{array}$$

2,000 is between 1,500 and 2,500. The third-grade students sold about 2,000 more candy bars than the fourth-grade students sold.

On Your Own

Andre earned $9.85 each week for 4 weeks. About how much money in all did Andre earn?

 Ⓐ About $20   Ⓒ About $40

 Ⓑ About $30   Ⓓ About $50

4. Make a Simpler Problem

Sometimes you can solve a problem by using smaller numbers. Then you can use the same method to help you solve the original problem.

Shawna numbered her paper from 1 through 40. How many times did she write the digit "2"? *2 12 20-29, 32, ~~40~~*

1, 1, 11, 1, 14

How to Do It

You can solve a simpler problem by finding the number of 2s in the ones and tens places. Remember when you write 22, the digit 2 is written twice.

Place Value	Number of 2s
1–9	1
10–19	1
20–29	11
30–39	1
40	+ 0
	Total: 14

Shawna wrote the digit "2" 14 times.

On Your Own

Tabitha typed the numbers 1 through 95 on her computer keyboard. How many times did she strike the digit "5"?

19

5   51   58
15   52   59
25   53   65
35   54   75
45   55   85
50   56   95
57

5. Write a Number Sentence

Writing a number sentence is another way to show the information in a problem. You can change the English words into a number sentence by using math signs.

English Words	Math Signs
is	equals (=)
in all, sum, increased by	addition (+)
decreased by, difference	subtraction (−)
of, product, times	multiplication (×)
each, per, quotient	division (÷)

SAMPLE PROBLEM

How many dogs are there in all? Write a number sentence to show the total number of dogs.

$4 \times 3 = 12$

How to Do It

The dogs are in groups of 3. There are 4 groups of 3. You can count by 3s to find the answer, or you can write a number sentence using multiplication.

Write a number sentence: $3 + 3 + 3 + 3 = 12$ or $4 \times 3 = 12$

There are a total of 12 dogs.

On Your Own

Marvin has 5 boxes of pencils. There are 8 pencils in each box. Write a number sentence to show the total number of pencils Marvin has in all.

40

6. Use a Formula

You can use a formula to solve a problem. A *formula* is a set of directions that you must follow. Once you know the formula, put the numbers from the problem into the formula. Then, add, subtract, multiply, or divide.

SAMPLE PROBLEM

What is the perimeter of this square?

6 × 4 = 24

24 ft.

6 ft.

6 ft.   6 ft.

6 ft.

How to Do It

The distance around a figure is called the *perimeter.* You can find the perimeter of any polygon by finding the sum of all the sides. All the sides of a square have the same length. Instead of adding the lengths of all the sides, you can use a formula to find the perimeter.

For a square, multiply 4 by the length of one side.

Perimeter of a square = 4 × 1 side

Perimeter = 4 × 6 ft.

Perimeter = 24 ft.

The perimeter of the square is 24 feet.

On Your Own

A square has a perimeter of 12 inches. What is the length of each side?

3 inches

7. Use a Definition or Rule

Sometimes you need to know a rule or definition to solve a problem in geometry or measurement.

SAMPLE PROBLEM

Which streets are parallel?

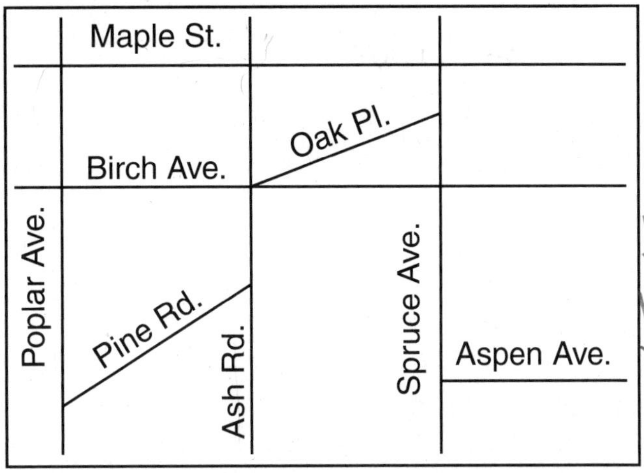

(handwritten list):
✓ Birch Ave.
✓ Maple St.
✓ Ash Rd.
✓ Poplar Ave.
✓ Spruce Ave.
✓ Aspen Ave

How to Do It

To solve this problem, you must use the definitions of parallel and intersecting lines.

Parallel lines are lines that never cross. The symbol for parallel is ∥.

Intersecting lines are lines that cross. The symbol for intersecting is ⊥.

Parallel Streets

Poplar Ave. ∥ Ash Rd.	Maple St. ∥ Birch Ave.
Poplar Ave. ∥ Spruce Ave.	Maple St. ∥ Aspen Ave.
Ash Rd. ∥ Spruce Ave.	Birch Ave. ∥ Aspen Ave.

On Your Own

Use the diagram above to name all the streets that intersect.

(handwritten):
Ash Rd.
Birch Ave.
Maple St.
Poplar Ave.
Spruce Ave.

(handwritten, right margin):
MS ⊥ AR
BA ⊥ AR
MS ⊥ SA
SA ⊥ AA
MS ⊥ SA

8. Work Backward

Some problems leave out the beginning information and give you only the answer. To solve these problems, you need to work backward.

Lisa traded baseball cards with her friends. On Friday, she had 11 cards in all. On Tuesday, Juan gave her 4 cards. On Wednesday, she gave away 2 cards. On Thursday, Bobby gave her 3 cards. How many cards did Lisa have on Monday?

How to Do It

Start with the number of baseball cards Lisa had on Friday. List the number of cards added or subtracted on each day.

Friday:	11	Wednesday:	−2
Thursday:	+3	Tuesday:	+4

Then work backward by changing the + signs to − signs and the − sign to a + sign.

Friday:	11 cards
Thursday:	11 − 3 = 8 cards
Wednesday:	8 + 2 = 10 cards
Tuesday:	10 − 4 = 6 cards
Monday:	6 cards

Lisa had 6 baseball cards on Monday. Check your answer by starting with 6 and adding and subtracting the number of cards for each day.

On Your Own

What number belongs in the *start* box?

28

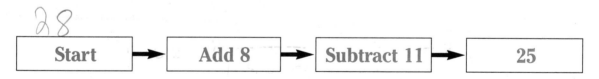

9. Use Logical Thinking

Sometimes you don't need to add, subtract, multiply, or divide. Instead, you can use logical thinking to solve problems. Logical thinking can help you make decisions and find the best choices.

SAMPLE PROBLEM

Mary, Keesha, Beth, and Rosa each have a pet. One girl has a dog, one has a cat, one has a bird, and one has a fish. Read the clues below and find which pet each girl has.

Clues: Mary has a pet that does not bark or purr.   *fish*

Keesha has a pet with four legs.   *cat*

Beth has a pet that begins with the same letter as her name.   *bird*

Rosa has a pet that likes to fetch and go for walks.   *dog*

How to Do It

Use a logic chart to solve this problem. After you read each clue, fill in the chart by writing *yes* or *no*.

	Dog	Cat	Bird	Fish
Mary	No	No	No	Yes
Keesha	No	Yes	No	No
Beth	No	No	Yes	No
Rosa	Yes	No	No	No

On Your Own

Micah, Josh, and Anthony have bikes that are different colors. One boy has a blue bike, one has a red bike, and one has a black bike. Read the clues below and find which boy has which color bike.

Clues: Micah does not have a black bike.   *blue*
Josh's bike is the same color as a stop sign.   *red*

Anthony black

NJ ASK Modeled Instruction
Numbers and Numerical Operations

SAMPLE PROBLEM

1. Dawn wants to buy a toy that costs $4.75. She has 3 quarters, 8 dimes, 10 nickels, and 7 pennies. Her sister gave her 3 one-dollar bills. Does Dawn have enough money to buy the toy?

$5.12   M5   155
        +80   +50
        155   205   212

How to Do It

Make a Chart, Graph, or List

Organize the value of each coin and bill in a chart.

Coins or Bills	Operation	Value of Coin or Bill		Total
3 quarters	×	$0.25	=	$0.75
8 dimes	×	$0.10	=	$0.80
10 nickels	×	$0.05	=	$0.50
7 pennies	×	$0.01	=	$0.07
3 one-dollar bills	×	$1.00	=	+ $3.00
			Find the total	$5.12

Dawn has enough money to buy the toy that costs $4.75.

On Your Own

The library sells rulers for 40¢ each and pencils for 15¢ each. On Thursday, the library sold 2 rulers and 9 pencils. What was the total sale?

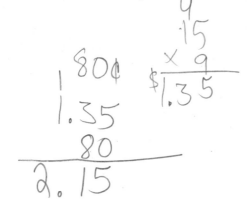

        4
       15
80¢   × 9
1.35 $1.35 $2.15
  80
2.15

New Jersey Mathematics Standards
1. **Numbers and Numerical Operations 4.1 B5** Count and perform simple computations with money.

2. **Find the sum of the place-value models.**

1

3 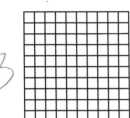 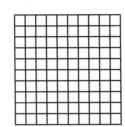 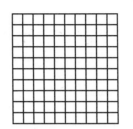 *2*  *7* *1*

+ *2* 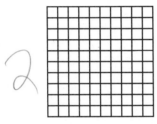 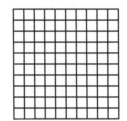 *8* 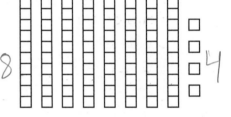 *4*

_____

3 *6* *2* *1* *1*

How to Do It

Use a place-value model to help you find the sum.

Hundreds	Tens	Ones
3	2	7
2	8	4

Find the sum: 327
          + 284
          611

On Your Own

Find the exact answer: 473 − 89

3 16 13
473
− 89
_____
384   ✓

New Jersey Mathematics Standards
2. **Numbers and Numerical Operations 4.1 A2** Demonstrate an understanding of whole number place value concepts and **4.1 B4** Use efficient and accurate pencil-and-paper procedures for computation with whole numbers.

3. **What is my name?**

   1. **My tens digit is five more than my hundreds digit.**

   2. **My thousands digit is four less than my ones digit.**

   3. **My hundreds digit is twice my thousands digit.**

   4. **My ones digit is 6.**

   2,4 9 6

How to Do It

Work Backward

Work backward to solve this problem.

The number has 4 digits.

Start with the ones digit: 6

The thousands digit is 4 less than the ones digit: $6 - 4 = 2$

The hundreds digit is twice the thousands digit: $2 \times 2 = 4$

The tens digit is 5 more than the hundreds digit: $4 + 5 = 9$

Thousands	Hundreds	Tens	Ones
2	4	9	6

My name is two-thousand four-hundred ninety-six.

On Your Own

What is my name? My tens digit is four times my ones digit. My hundreds digit is half of my tens digit. My ones digit is 2.

362

New Jersey Mathematics Standards
3. **Numbers and Numerical Operations 4.1 A2** Demonstrate an understanding of whole number place value concepts and **4.1 B1** Develop the meanings of the four basic arithmetic operations by modeling a large variety of problems.

SAMPLE PROBLEM

4. Alexis washed cars for 3 hours on Friday and 6 hours on Saturday. She earns $5 per hour. How much money did she earn in all?

$45

How to Do It

Write a Number Sentence

Find the total number of hours Alexis washed cars.

Write a number sentence:

Total Hours = Friday Hours + Saturday Hours

Friday:	3 hours
Saturday:	+ 6 hours
Total	9 hours

Find the total earnings. Multiply the total hours by the amount of money she earns per hour.

Write a number sentence:

Total Earnings = total hours × hourly earnings

Total Earnings:	9 total hours
	× $ 5 per hour
	$45

Alexis earned $45 in all.

On Your Own

Janice practices ice skating 1 hour before school and 3 hours after school. She does this 5 days a week. How many hours in all does she practice in 1 week?

20 hr.

New Jersey Mathematics Standards
4. **Numbers and Numerical Operations 4.1 A1** Use real-life experiences to construct meanings for numbers and **4.1 B1** Develop the meanings of the four basic arithmetic operations by modeling a large variety of problems.

5. A box of cereal is $\frac{7}{8}$ full. Another box is $\frac{3}{4}$ full. Which box has more cereal?
    Compare the boxes using $<$, $>$, or $=$.

$$\frac{7}{8} > \frac{3}{4}$$

How to Do It

Draw a Picture

You can draw a picture to compare fractions.

Draw a box and divide it into eighths.

Shade in $\frac{7}{8}$ of the box.

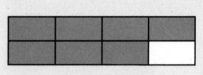

Draw the same box and divide it into fourths.

Shade in $\frac{3}{4}$ of the box.

Compare the two pictures using the signs:

$<$ less than $>$ greater than $=$ equals

$\frac{7}{8} > \frac{3}{4}$ or $\frac{3}{4} < \frac{7}{8}$ The box that is $\frac{7}{8}$ full has more cereal.

On Your Own

A box of crackers is $\frac{2}{3}$ full. Another box is $\frac{5}{6}$ full. Which box has more crackers?
Draw a picture and use $<$, $>$, or $=$ to explain your answer.

$$\frac{2}{3} < \frac{5}{6}$$

New Jersey Mathematics Standards
5. **Numbers and Numerical Operations 4.1 A1** Use real-life experiences to construct
    meanings for numbers and **4.1 A6** Compare and order numbers.

6. Nadia bought 1 dozen cookies. She gave $\frac{1}{2}$ of them to her friend and 2 to her teacher. How many cookies does Nadia have left? 4

How to Do It

Use a Definition or Rule

To solve this problem, you must know the definition of one dozen.

One dozen = 12

Find the number of cookies Nadia gave to her friend:

$\frac{1}{2} \times 12 = 6$

Add the number of cookies she gave to her friend and her teacher:

Friend	6
Teacher	+ 2
Total	8

Find the number of cookies Nadia has left.

$$\begin{array}{r} 12 \\ -\ 8 \\ \hline 4 \end{array}$$

Nadia has 4 cookies left.

On Your Own

Thomas bought 2 dozen pencils. He gave $\frac{1}{4}$ of them to his brother and 5 to his cousin. How many pencils does Thomas have left? 13

New Jersey Mathematics Standards
6. **Numbers and Numerical Operations 4.1 A1** Use real-life experiences to construct meanings for numbers and **4.1 A5** Understand the various uses of numbers.

7. Estimate the product of 28 × 21. The product is between what two numbers?

Ⓐ 450 and 550

Ⓑ 550 and 650

Ⓒ 650 and 750

Ⓓ 750 and 850

How to Do It

Estimate

You can round both numbers and estimate the product.

Round each number to the nearest ten.

28 rounds up to 30.

21 rounds to 20.

Find the product: 30
            × 20
            600

600 is between 550 and 650. The answer is B.

On Your Own

Estimate the difference of 892 − 415. The difference is between what two numbers?

Ⓐ 250 and 350

Ⓑ 350 and 450

Ⓒ 450 and 550

Ⓓ 550 and 650

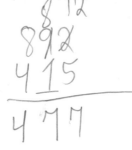

New Jersey Mathematics Standards
7. **Numbers and Numerical Operations 4.1 C2** Construct and use a variety of estimation strategies (e.g., rounding and mental math) for estimating both quantities and the result of computations.

PRACTICE PROBLEM

1. Keiko is counting the number of windows on the front of a building, but a tree is in her way.

If there are 12 windows on the front of the building, how many windows are covered by the tree?

Ⓐ **5**

Ⓑ **7**

Ⓒ **10**

Ⓓ **12**

🌀 **Tip:** Count the number of windows Keiko can see. Then subtract this number from the total number of windows.

New Jersey Mathematics Standards
1. **Numbers and Numerical Operations 4.1 A5** Understand the various uses of numbers.

2. Mrs. Lopez had $646 in the bank. She put another $335 in the bank. How much money does she have in the bank now?

   Ⓐ $311

   Ⓑ $911

   Ⓒ $971

   Ⓓ $981

   Ⓖ **Tip:** The problem asks you to find the total of two amounts. Use addition to find how much money Mrs. Lopez has in the bank now. Remember to line up the ones column before you add.

3. Hannah has 84 star stickers. She gives 8 stickers to Courtney, 6 stickers to Elton, and 14 stickers to Javier. How many stickers does Hannah have left?

   Ⓐ 114

   Ⓑ 76

   Ⓒ 56

   Ⓓ 39

   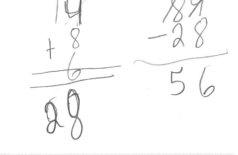

   Ⓖ **Tip:** Every time Hannah gives some stickers away, she has fewer stickers. She began with 84 stickers. Use subtraction to take away from her total.

   New Jersey Mathematics Standards
   2. **Numbers and Numerical Operations 4.1 B4** Use efficient and accurate pencil-and-paper procedures for computation with whole numbers.
   3. **Numbers and Numerical Operations 4.1 B1** Develop the meanings of the four basic arithmetic operations by modeling and discussing a large variety of problems.

PRACTICE PROBLEMS

4. **Which list shows the numbers in order from least to greatest?**

   Ⓐ 865, 839, 761

   Ⓑ 839, 865, 761

   Ⓒ 761, 865, 839

   Ⓓ 761, 839, 865

   🌀 **Tip:** Compare the numbers starting with the greatest place value, hundreds: 8̲65, 8̲39, 7̲61. Since 7 is less than 8, 761 is the least number. Now compare the tens place of the other two numbers: 86̲5 and 83̲9. Since 3 is less than 6, 839 is the lesser number. Now list the numbers from least to greatest.

5. **During one basketball season, Danny shot 343 free throws. He made 301 of the free throws. How many times did he miss?**

   Ⓐ 868

   Ⓑ 826

   Ⓒ 68

   Ⓓ 42

   🌀 **Tip:** The problem asks you to find the difference between two amounts. Use subtraction to find the difference between the number of free throws shot, 343, and the number of free throws made, 301.

New Jersey Mathematics Standards
4. **Numbers and Numerical Operations 4.1 A6** Compare and order numbers.
5. **Numbers and Numerical Operations 4.1 B4** Use efficient and accurate pencil-and-paper procedures for computation with whole numbers.

6. Which circle is $\frac{4}{6}$ shaded?

Ⓐ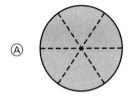

Ⓑ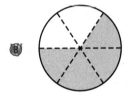

Ⓒ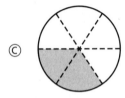

Ⓓ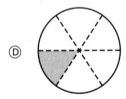

🌀 **Tip:** Remember that the top number, the numerator, stands for the parts of the circle that are shaded. The bottom number, the denominator, stands for the total parts of the circle. Each circle is divided into 6 equal parts. Find the circle that has 4 of these parts shaded.

New Jersey Mathematics Standards
6. **Numbers and Numerical Operations 4.1 A1** Use real-life experiences, physical materials, and technology to construct meanings for numbers.

7. **Which number is an even number?**

   Ⓐ 9

   Ⓑ 12

   Ⓒ 27

   Ⓓ 35

   Ⓢ **Tip:** For a number to be even, its last digit must be 0, 2, 4, 6, or 8.

8. **How much will 2 long-sleeve shirts and 1 sweater cost?**

SALE			
Short-Sleeve Shirt	$10	Sweater	$40
Long-Sleeve Shirt	$25	Jacket	$55

   Ⓐ $45

   Ⓑ $60

   Ⓒ $90

   Ⓓ $105

   Ⓢ **Tip:** This is a two-step problem. First find the cost of the 2 long-sleeve shirts. Use addition, $25 + $25, or use multiplication, $25 × 2. Then add the cost of the sweater to the cost of the 2 long-sleeve shirts.

New Jersey Mathematics Standards
7. **Numbers and Numerical Operations 4.1 A3** Identify whether any whole number is odd or even.
8. **Numbers and Numerical Operations 4.1 B1** Develop the meanings of the four basic arithmetic operations by modeling and discussing a large variety of problems.

9. What is the value of the 3 in 14.38?

   Ⓐ thirty

   Ⓑ three

   Ⓒ three tenths

   Ⓓ three hundredths

   🌀 **Tip:** The digit 3 is to the right of the decimal point. Its value is less than 1. The decimal places start on the right of the decimal point. Remember the values of the decimal places from left to right are: tenths, hundredths. The digit 3 is in the first place to the right of the decimal point.

10. Phillip bought 7 packages of canned peaches. Each package had 4 cans. How many cans of peaches did he buy in all?

    Ⓐ 11

    Ⓑ 24

    Ⓒ 28

    Ⓓ 35

    🌀 **Tip:** One way to find the total is to add: 4 + 4 + 4 + 4 + 4 + 4 + 4. Knowing the multiplication fact 4 × 7 makes the problem easier: 4 cans per package × 7 packages = ___ cans.

New Jersey Mathematics Standards
9. **Numbers and Numerical Operations 4.1 A4** Explore the extension of the place value system to decimals through hundredths.
10. **Numbers and Numerical Operations 4.1 B3** Construct, use, and explain procedures for performing whole number calculations.

PRACTICE PROBLEM

$1.75

11.

Which group shows the same amount of money as shown above?

Ⓐ  $1.25

Ⓑ  $1.50

Ⓒ  $1.65

Ⓓ  $1.75

🎯 **Tip:** Remember the values of the bills and coins. A dollar bill = 100¢, a quarter = 25¢, a dime = 10¢, and a nickel = 5¢. Find the value of the money in the problem:
100¢ + 25¢ + 25¢ + 10¢ + 10¢ + 5¢ = 175¢.
Then find the group that shows the same amount of money.

New Jersey Mathematics Standards
11. Numbers and Numerical Operations 4.1 B5 Count and perform simple computations with money.

12. Tamika has 15 pieces of gum to give to her 5 friends. She will give each friend the same number of pieces. How many pieces of gum will Tamika give each friend?

Ⓐ 15

Ⓑ 10

Ⓒ   5

Ⓓ   3

Ⓢ **Tip:** Tamika will share a total of 15 pieces of gum equally. Sharing usually means to divide. Remember that division is the opposite of multiplication. Use the multiplication fact 3 × 5 to help you solve the problem.

13. **What is the value of the 5 in 37,592?**

Ⓐ five hundred

Ⓑ fifty

Ⓒ five

Ⓓ five tenths

Ⓢ **Tip:** The value of a digit depends on its place in a number. Remember the values of the *whole number* places from *right to left* are: ones, tens, hundreds, thousands, ten thousands. The digit 5 is in the third place to the left.

New Jersey Mathematics Standards

12. **Numbers and Numerical Operations 4.1 B2** Develop proficiency with basic multiplication and division number facts using a variety of fact strategies (such as "skip counting" and "repeated subtraction").

13. **Numbers and Numerical Operations 4.1 A2** Demonstrate an understanding of whole number place value concepts.

PRACTICE PROBLEM

14. There are 8 sections in the circle: 3 blue sections, 1 green section, 2 red sections, and 2 yellow sections.

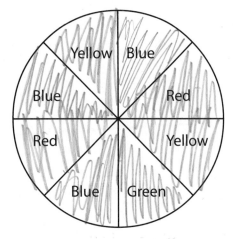

What fraction of the sections are red?

Ⓐ $\dfrac{5}{8}$

Ⓑ $\dfrac{3}{8}$

Ⓒ $\dfrac{2}{8}$

Ⓓ $\dfrac{1}{8}$

🌀 **Tip:** Find the number of sections that are red. This is the numerator. The total number of sections is the denominator.

New Jersey Mathematics Standards
14. **Numbers and Numerical Operations 4.1 A1** Use real-life experiences, physical materials, and technology to construct meanings for numbers.

15. Estimate 341 + 608. The sum is between which numbers?

Ⓐ 600 and 700

Ⓑ 700 and 800

Ⓒ 800 and 900

Ⓓ 900 and 1,000

> **☺ Tip:** One way to estimate is to round both numbers and then add. Round each number to the nearest hundred and then find the sum of the numbers.

16. Mr. Garcia worked 6 hours a day for 4 days. Then he worked 8 hours a day for 2 days. How many hours did he work in these 6 days?

Ⓐ 16

Ⓑ 24

Ⓒ 40

Ⓓ 44

> **☺ Tip:** Find the number of hours Mr. Garcia worked in four 6-hour days. Then find the number of hours he worked in two 8-hour days. Add the two sums to find the total amount of time he worked in 6 days.

New Jersey Mathematics Standards
15. **Numbers and Numerical Operations 4.1 C2** Construct and use a variety of estimation strategies (e.g., rounding and mental math) for estimating both quantities and the result of computations.
16. **Numbers and Numerical Operations 4.1 B1** Develop the meanings of the four basic arithmetic operations by modeling and discussing a large variety of problems.

PRACTICE PROBLEM

DIRECTIONS: The following questions are open-ended questions. Write your answer and show your work in the space following each problem.

17. There are 6 boxes in the corner of the classroom. There are 12 workbooks in half of the boxes and 10 workbooks in the rest of the boxes. The teacher needs 80 workbooks for her students.

    • How many more workbooks does the teacher need?

    • Use words and pictures to show how you solved the problem.

🌀 **Tip:** First find the total number of workbooks in the 6 boxes. Remember, the boxes have different numbers of workbooks in them. Then find the difference between the total number of workbooks in the boxes and the total number of workbooks needed.

New Jersey Mathematics Standards
17. **Numbers and Numerical Operations 4.1 A1** Use real-life experiences, physical materials, and technology to construct meanings for numbers and **4.1 B4** use efficient and accurate pencil-and-paper procedures for computation with whole numbers.

18. Bookcase 1 has 5 shelves. There are 15 books on each shelf. Bookcase 2 has 8 shelves. There are 12 books on each shelf.

- Which bookcase has more books?

- Show all your work and explain your answer.

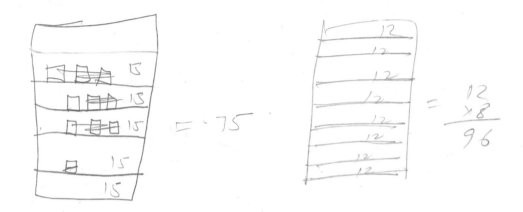

🌀 **Tip:** The problem asks you to compare two amounts: the number of books in bookcase 1 and the number of books in bookcase 2. There are two ways to find the number of books in each bookcase. You can add the number of books on each shelf. You also can multiply the number of books on each shelf by the number of shelves.

New Jersey Mathematics Standards
18. **Numbers and Numerical Operations 4.1 A1** Use real-life experiences, physical materials, and technology to construct meanings for numbers and **4.1 B4** Use efficient and accurate pencil-and-paper procedures for computation with whole numbers.

Lesson 3

NJ ASK Modeled Instruction
Geometry

1. How many line segments are there in this figure? 2

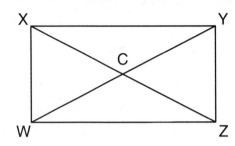

How to Do It

Use a Definition or Rule

A line goes on forever in each direction. A line can be named by any two points on the line.

This is read as *line FG*.
Another way to write this is $\overleftrightarrow{FG}$.

A line segment is part of a line. A line segment has two endpoints.

This is read as *line segment JK*.
Another way to write this is $\overline{JK}$.

A ray has an endpoint on one side. On the other side, it goes on forever, like a line.

This is read as *ray PQ*.
Another way to write this is $\overrightarrow{PQ}$.

Name all the line segments in the figure.

$\overline{WX}$ $\overline{XY}$ $\overline{YZ}$ $\overline{ZW}$ $\overline{WC}$ $\overline{CY}$ $\overline{WY}$ $\overline{XC}$ $\overline{CZ}$ $\overline{XZ}$

On Your Own

Name all the line segments, rays, and lines in this figure.

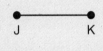

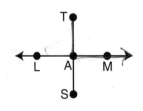

New Jersey Mathematics Standards
1. **Geometry 4.2 A4** Understand and apply concepts involving lines, angles, and circles.

2. Look at the figure below. Draw an example of a slide, flip, and turn.

How to Do It

Sort the Data

The sliding, flipping, or turning of a figure is called a *transformation*. Use each definition below to draw the transformation.

Slide: A *slide* is made by moving the figure up, down, left, or right.

Flip: A *flip* gives a mirror image of the figure.

Turn: A *turn* turns the figure.

On Your Own

Name and draw three different transformations for this figure.

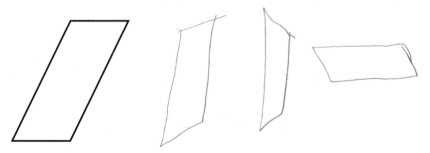

New Jersey Mathematics Standards
2. **Geometry 4.2 B1** Describe and use geometric transformations (slide, flip, turn).

3. Place these ordered pairs on the grid: (2,6), (5,1), (5,11), (8,6). Connect the points. Draw a line of symmetry.

How to Do It

Use Logical Thinking

To plot an ordered pair, move the first number along the horizontal scale. Then move the second number along the vertical scale. Connect the points. Draw a line of symmetry. A figure has symmetry if both halves are the same. This figure has two lines of symmetry.

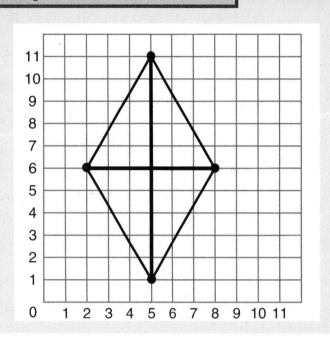

On Your Own

Place these ordered pairs on the grid: (3,6), (3,10), (8,6). Connect the points. Flip the figure over the line of symmetry. Name the ordered pairs that will complete the other half of the figure.

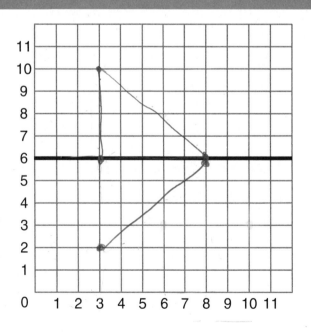

New Jersey Mathematics Standards
3. **Geometry 4.2 A3** Identify and describe relationships among two-dimensional shapes and
  4.2 C1 Locate and name points in the first quadrant on a coordinate grid.

4. **What type of angle is shown by each clock?**

180°   obtuce   acute   right

| Clock 1 | Clock 2 | Clock 3 | Clock 4 |

How to Do It

Use a Definition or Rule

The sign for an angle is "∠". This angle can be written as ∠ABC:

A right angle has a measure of 90 degrees.

It has the shape of a square corner.

An acute angle is less than 90 degrees.

An obtuse angle is greater than 90 degrees.

A straight angle has a measure of 180 degrees.
It has the shape of a straight line.

| Clock 1 | Clock 2 | Clock 3 | Clock 4 |
| straight angle | obtuse angle | acute angle | right angle |

On Your Own

Name all the right, acute, and, obtuse angles in this figure.

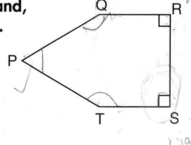

right   ∠QRS
R S T Q P

right

This page may not be reproduced without permission of Harcourt Achieve.

New Jersey Mathematics Standards
4. **Geometry 4.2 A4** Understand and apply concepts involving lines, angles, and circles.

SAMPLE PROBLEM

5. How many rectangles are in this figure?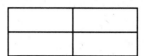

How to Do It

Use a Definition or Rule

A rectangle is an example of a *polygon*. Polygons are classified by the number of sides they have.

triangle	square	rectangle	pentagon	hexagon

Number of sides   3   4   4   5   6

Look for all four-sided, rectangular polygons in the figure.

1	2
3	4

5	6

7
8

9

There are 9 rectangles in the figure.

On Your Own

How many triangles are in this figure?

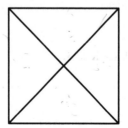

New Jersey Mathematics Standards
5. **Geometry 4.2 A2** Use properties of standard three-dimensional and two-dimensional
shapes to identify, classify, and describe them.

6. **Name and count all the space figures in this drawing.**

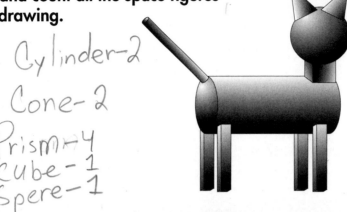

(handwritten) 10

Cylinder-2
Cone-2
Prism-4
Cube-1
Spere-1

How to Do It

Make a Chart, Graph, or List

Space figures have faces, corners, and edges:

corner
edge
face

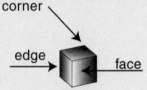 

Cube   Rectangular Prism   Cylinder   Cone   Pyramid   Sphere

Count and list all the space figures in the drawing.

Cube = 1   Rectangular Prism = 4   Cylinder = 2   Cone = 2   Sphere = 1

On Your Own

A face is a flat side of a figure. How many faces does each space figure have? Complete the chart.

Space Figure	Number of Faces
Cube	6
Rectangular Prism	6
Cylinder	2
Cone	1
Pyramid	5
Sphere	0

New Jersey Mathematics Standards
6. **Geometry 4.2 A2** Use properties of standard three-dimensional and two-dimensional shapes to identify, classify, and describe them.

7. Look at these drawings. What does this figure look like?

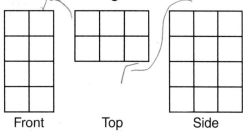

Front   Top   Side

How to Do It

Draw a Picture

A figure looks different from the front, top, and side. You can use manipulatives to help you draw this figure. First draw the front view, then the top, and finally the side.

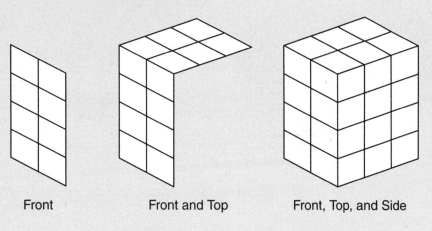

Front   Front and Top   Front, Top, and Side

On Your Own

Draw the front, top, and side views of this figure.

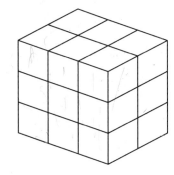

New Jersey Mathematics Standards
7. **Geometry 4.2 A5** Recognize, describe, extend, and create space-filling patterns.

1. **Which of the following describes the change from Figure 1 to Figure 2?**

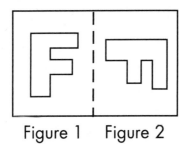

Figure 1   Figure 2

Ⓐ **turn left**

Ⓑ **turn right**

Ⓒ **flip**

Ⓓ **slide**

☉ Tip: When a figure is flipped over a line, its mirror, or opposite, image is shown. A slide moves the figure up, down, left, or right. A turn moves a figure around a point, like the hands on a clock.

New Jersey Mathematics Standards
1. **Geometry 4.2 B1** Describe and use geometric transformations (slide, flip, turn).

PRACTICE PROBLEM

2. **Which model shows a line segment?**

Ⓐ

Ⓑ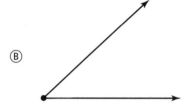

Ⓒ

Ⓓ

🌀 **Tip:** A line segment is a part of a line. A line segment has 2 endpoints that show where the segment begins and ends. A line is straight. It has arrows on both ends to show that it goes on in both directions. A line can have one or more points on it.

New Jersey Mathematics Standards
2. Geometry 4.2 A4 Understand and apply concepts involving lines, angles, and circles.

3. Doug's teacher put this pattern of shapes on the classroom floor.

If Doug stands on the triangle facing the pentagon, what shape is behind him?

Ⓐ

Ⓑ

Ⓒ

Ⓓ

🌀 **Tip:** If Doug is facing the pentagon, he can look to his left and see 1 shape. He can look to his right and see 2 shapes. From the triangle, Doug can see all the shapes except the one behind him.

New Jersey Mathematics Standards
3. Geometry 4.2 A1 Identify and describe spatial relationships of two or more objects in space.

PRACTICE PROBLEM

4. **Which figure is the same size and shape as Shape K?**

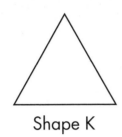

Shape K

Ⓐ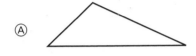

Ⓑ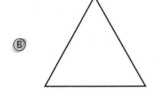

Ⓒ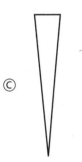

Ⓓ

🌀 **Tip:** Shape K is a triangle. Its sides are equal in length. Find the triangle that has sides that are the same length as the sides of Shape K.

New Jersey Mathematics Standards
4. **Geometry 4.2 A1** Identify and describe spatial relationships of two or more objects in space.

5. **Which figure below has more than 1 line of symmetry?**

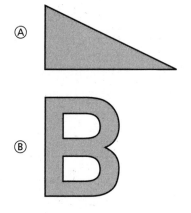

A

B

C

D

🌀 **Tip:** A line of symmetry divides a figure into two matching parts. If a figure is folded along a line of symmetry, the halves will match exactly. Some figures have 0 lines of symmetry or 1 line of symmetry. Others have 2 or many lines of symmetry.

This page may not be reproduced without permission of Harcourt Achieve.

New Jersey Mathematics Standards
5. **Geometry 4.2 A3** Identify and describe relationships among two-dimensional shapes.

PRACTICE PROBLEM

6. Justin made this pattern.

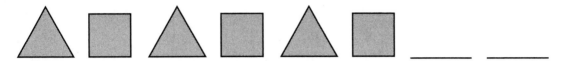

What are the next two shapes in the pattern?

Ⓐ

Ⓑ

Ⓒ

Ⓓ

🌀 **Tip:** The pattern used two shapes: a triangle and a square. The square always comes after the triangle. The part of the pattern shown ends with a square. Continue the pattern by adding the next two shapes.

New Jersey Mathematics Standards
6. Geometry 4.2 A5 Recognize, describe, extend, and create space-filling patterns.

7. Which figure has 1 square face?

(A)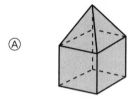

(B)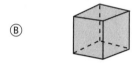

(C)

(D)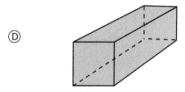

🌀 **Tip:** The face of a figure is one of its flat surfaces. The dashed lines on the figures show the shapes of the faces that cannot be seen from the front. Find the figure with only 1 square face. All four figures have at least 1 square face.

New Jersey Mathematics Standards
7. **Geometry 4.2 A2** Use properties of standard three-dimensional and two-dimensional shapes to identify, classify, and describe them.

PRACTICE PROBLEM

8. **Which object is shaped like a cone?**

Ⓐ

Ⓑ
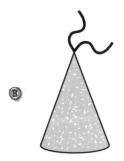

Ⓒ
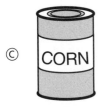

Ⓓ
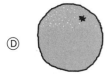

🌀 **Tip:** A cone has 1 flat surface that is shaped like a circle.

This page may not be reproduced without permission of Harcourt Achieve.

New Jersey Mathematics Standards

8. **Geometry 4.2 A2** Use properties of standard three-dimensional and two-dimensional shapes to identify, classify, and describe them.

9. Which point is located at (4, 8)?

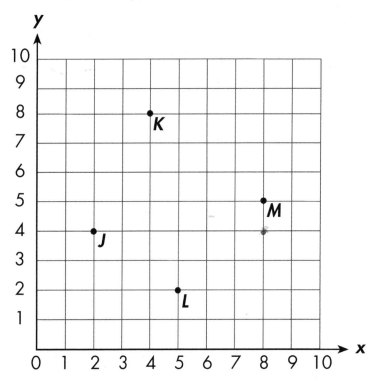

Ⓐ **J**

Ⓑ **K**

Ⓒ **L**

Ⓓ **M**

🌀 **Tip:** The numbers (4, 8) are an ordered pair. They tell where a point is on the grid. The first number tells how far the point is to the right. The second number tells how far the point is up. To find the point at (4, 8), start at (0, 0) on the grid. Count 4 spaces to the right and then count 8 spaces up.

New Jersey Mathematics Standards
9. Geometry 4.2 C1 Locate and name points in the first quadrant on a coordinate grid.

Lesson 4

NJ ASK Modeled Instruction
Measurement

SAMPLE PROBLEM

1. **Find the perimeter of this polygon.**

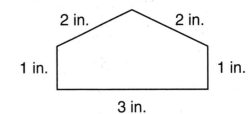

2 in.   2 in.

1 in.   1 in.

3 in.

9 in

How to Do It

Use a Definition or Rule

To find the perimeter of any polygon, add all the sides. This polygon is called a pentagon. It has five sides.

Perimeter = 2 in. + 1 in. + 3 in. + 1 in. + 2 in.

Perimeter = 9 in.

On Your Own

Find the perimeter of this polygon.

4 ft.

3 ft.   3 ft.

2 ft.   2 ft.

3 ft.   3 ft.

2 ft.   2 ft.

3 ft.   3 ft.

4 ft.

34 ft

New Jersey Mathematics Standards
1. **Measurement 4.2 E2** Determine the perimeter of simple shapes by measuring all of the sides.

2. **How many miles is the park from the school?**

$5\dfrac{3}{4}$

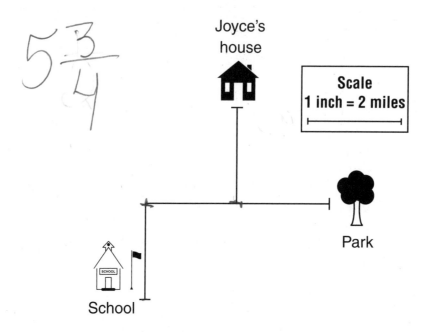

Joyce's house

Scale
1 inch = 2 miles

Park

School

How to Do It

Compute/Use Manipulatives

Use your ruler to measure the distance from the park to the school. The distance is 3 inches. Use the scale 1 inch = 2 miles to change inches to miles.

Multiply 3 inches by 2 miles.

$$\begin{array}{r} 3 \\ \times\ 2 \\ \hline 6 \text{ miles} \end{array}$$

The park is 6 miles from the school.

On Your Own

How many miles is it from Joyce's house to the school? 6

New Jersey Mathematics Standards
2. **Measurement 4.2 D2** Select and use appropriate standard units of measure and measurement tools to solve real-life problems.

SAMPLE PROBLEM

3. **Which can is heavier? Use <, >, or = in the ☐.**

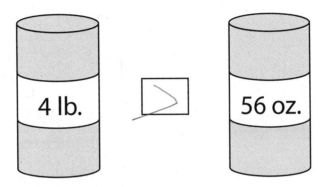

How to Do It

Use Logical Thinking

There are 16 ounces in 1 pound. Change 4 pounds to ounces. To change pounds to ounces, multiply by 16.

4 lb. = ? oz.

$$\begin{array}{r} 16 \\ \times\ 4 \\ \hline 64\ \text{oz.} \end{array}$$

4 lb. = 64 oz.

64 oz. > 56 oz.

On Your Own

Each can is the same size and shape. Which can is the heaviest?

paper clips

Ⓐ

rocks

Ⓑ

pencils

Ⓒ

cotton balls

Ⓓ

New Jersey Mathematics Standards

3. **Measurement 4.2 D3** Incorporate estimation in measurement activities (e.g., estimate before measuring).

4. Find the area and perimeter of this figure.

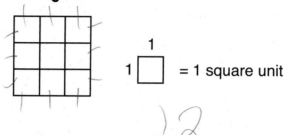

1 [ ] = 1 square unit

How to Do It

Compute/Use Manipulatives

To find the area, count the number of square units.

1	2	3
4	5	6
7	8	9

The area is 9 square units.

To find the perimeter, count the units around the figure.

The perimeter is 12 units.

On Your Own

Draw a rectangular figure with an area of 12 square units and a perimeter of 14 units.

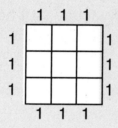

New Jersey Mathematics Standards
4. **Measurement 4.2 E1** Determine the area of simple two-dimensional shapes on a square grid and **4.2 E2** Determine the perimeter of simple shapes by measuring all of the sides.

SAMPLE PROBLEM

5. Nicholas is going to Ahmed's birthday party. Nicholas leaves his house at 1:30 p.m. It will take Nicholas 22 minutes to walk to Ahmed's house. On the way to the birthday party, Nicholas must make a few stops. First, he must stop at the toy store to get Ahmed a gift. This will take 23 minutes. Then he must wait for the gift to be wrapped. This will take 14 minutes. Finally, he must go to the card shop to buy a card to go with the gift. This will take 11 minutes. What time will Nicholas arrive at Ahmed's house?

(handwritten: 22, 23, +14, 11, 70 min., 2:40pm)

How to Do It: **Make a Chart, Graph, or List**

You can solve the problem by making a list of the activities and the time it takes Nicholas to complete each one.

Activity	Time (minutes)
Walk to Ahmed's House	22
Go to Toy Store	23
Get Gift Wrapped	14
Go to Card Shop	+11
Total	70 minutes

Remember:

60 seconds = 1 minute

60 minutes = 1 hour

24 hours = 1 day

Change 70 minutes to hours: 70 minutes = 1 hour 10 minutes

Add 1 hour 10 minutes to 1:30 P.M.

Nicholas will arrive at Ahmed's house at 2:40 P.M.

On Your Own

Tina arrived at the bowling alley at the time shown on clock 1. She left the bowling alley at the time shown on clock 2. How long was she at the bowling alley?

Clock 1

Clock 2

(handwritten: 1:15)

New Jersey Mathematics Standards

5. **Measurement 4.2 D1** Understand that everyday objects have a variety of attributes, each of which can be measured in many ways.

6. **Which figure has the greater volume?**

Figure A   Figure B

How to Do It

Compute/Use Manipulatives

To find the volume of a space figure, count the number of cubic units in the figure.

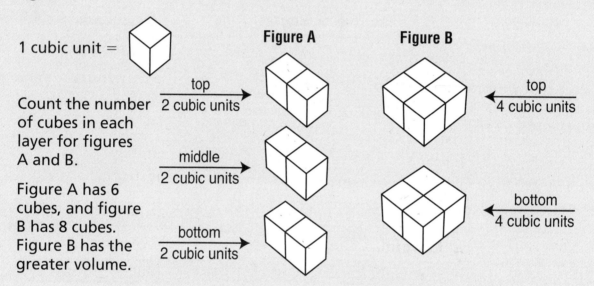

1 cubic unit =

Count the number of cubes in each layer for figures A and B.

Figure A has 6 cubes, and figure B has 8 cubes. Figure B has the greater volume.

Figure A

top
2 cubic units

middle
2 cubic units

bottom
2 cubic units

Figure B

top
4 cubic units

bottom
4 cubic units

On Your Own

What is the volume of the figure below?

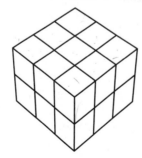

New Jersey Mathematics Standards

6. **Measurement 4.2 E3** Measure and compare the volume of three-dimensional objects using materials such as rice or cubes.

SAMPLE PROBLEM

7. Cole read the temperature on the thermometer before he went to bed. When he woke up, the temperature was 8 degrees colder. What is the new temperature?

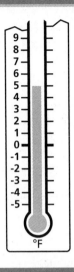

How to Do It

Compute/Use Manipulatives

To read the temperature, look at the mark beside the top of the shaded column: 5°F

Start at 5 degrees and count down 8 marks.

Read the new temperature: −3°F

On Your Own

Shade the thermometers to show these temperatures. Then list the temperatures in order from coldest to warmest.

1 −4°F   *4* 6°F   *2* −1°F   *3* 4°F

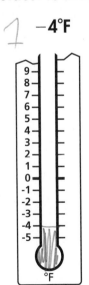 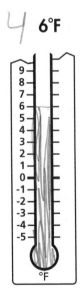 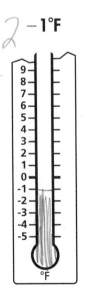 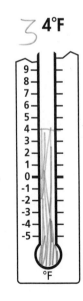

New Jersey Mathematics Standards
7. **Measurement 4.2 D1** Understand that everyday objects have a variety of attributes, each of which can be measured in many ways.

1. On which object can Emilio make these three measurements: length, width, and height?

Ⓐ a bike tire

Ⓑ a large book

Ⓒ a can of soup

Ⓓ a sheet of paper

> 🌀 **Tip:** Length, width, and height all measure straight-line distances. Flat objects have only length and width. Solid objects that have faces with 4 sides have length, width, and height. Objects that are round or that have round faces do not have both length and width.

I got cunfused

New Jersey Mathematics Standards
1. **Measurement 4.2 D1** Understand that everyday objects have a variety of attributes, each of which can be measured in many ways.

PRACTICE PROBLEM

2. Each unit on the grid is 1 square inch. What is the area of the shaded part of the grid?

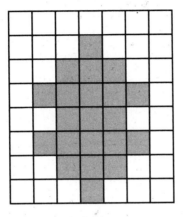

Ⓐ **29 square inches**

Ⓑ **24 square inches**

Ⓔ **21 square inches**

Ⓓ **12 square inches**

🔎 **Tip:** Remember that area measures the number of square units that cover a figure. To find the area of the shaded part of the grid, count the number of shaded squares.

This page may not be reproduced without permission of Harcourt Achieve.

New Jersey Mathematics Standards

2. **Measurement 4.2 E1** Determine the area of simple two-dimensional shapes on a square grid.

3. One ounce is the best unit to describe the weight of which object?

Ⓐ a slice of bread

Ⓑ a table

Ⓒ a car

Ⓓ an eyelash

Ⓢ **Tip:** A strawberry and a pencil both weigh about 1 ounce. Find the object that is most likely to weigh about the same amount as a strawberry or a pencil.

4. Which of these correctly states the area of a picture with a length of 5 inches and a width of 3 inches?

Ⓐ 15

Ⓑ 15 inches

Ⓒ 15 square inches

Ⓓ 15 cubic inches

Ⓢ **Tip:** Area measures the number of square units that will cover an object. One square unit is a square that is 1 unit long and 1 unit wide. Always write an area in square units. In this problem, the unit of measure is inches.

New Jersey Mathematics Standards
3. **Measurement 4.2 D2** Select and use appropriate standard units of measure and measurement tools to solve real-life problems.
4. **Measurement 4.2 D2** Select and use appropriate standard units of measure and measurement tools to solve real-life problems.

PRACTICE PROBLEM

5. **Inez needs to measure the weight of an apple. Which tool should she use to measure this weight?**

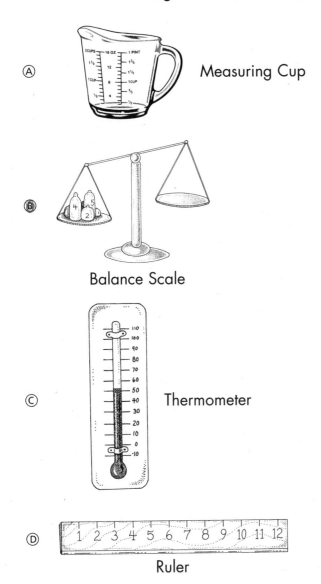

Ⓐ Measuring Cup

Ⓑ Balance Scale

Ⓒ Thermometer

Ⓓ

1 2 3 4 5 6 7 8 9 10 11 12

Ruler

🌀 **Tip:** Weight is how heavy an object is. The measuring cup measures capacity, or how much something holds. The balance scale measures weight. The thermometer measures temperature, or how hot or cold something is. The ruler measures length.

New Jersey Mathematics Standards
5. **Measurement 4.2 D2** Select and use appropriate standard units of measure and measurement tools to solve real-life problems.

DIRECTIONS: The following question is an open-ended question. Write your answer and show your work. You may use your calculator.

6. Brad built the figure below from unit cubes.

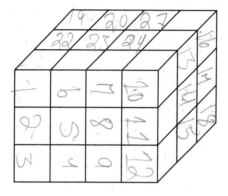

• **What is the volume of Brad's figure? Explain your answer.**

• **How many unit cubes in Brad's figure can you *see*?**

🌀 **Tip:** Volume is always written as cubic units. Brad's figure is made from unit cubes. Its volume equals the number of unit cubes in the figure. There are some unit cubes in the figure that you cannot see.

New Jersey Mathematics Standards
6. **Measurement 4.2 E3** Measure and compare the volume of three-dimensional objects using materials such as rice or cubes.

Lesson 5

NJ ASK Modeled Instruction
Patterns and Algebra

1. If 12 is subtracted from this number, the difference is 8. When this number is added to 11, the sum is 31. Find the number.

How to Do It

Write a Number Sentence

You should know the operations for the following words:

Words	Operation
sum, total, plus, more than	+
difference, subtracted from, less than	−
product, multiplied by	×
quotient, divided by	÷

Write a number sentence for each situation.

If 12 is subtracted from this number, the difference is 8.　　$? - 12 = 8$

When this number is added to 11, the sum is 31.　　$11 + ? = 31$

Find the missing number.

The number is 20.

On Your Own

The sum of 4 and this number is 12. When this number is subtracted from 17, the difference is 9. Find the number.

$4 + ? = 12$
$17 - ? = 9$

New Jersey Mathematics Standards
1. **Patterns and Algebra 4.3 C2** Construct and solve simple open sentences involving addition or subtraction (e.g., $3 + 6 = \_\_$, $n = 15 - 3$, $3 + \_\_ = 3$, $16 - c = 7$).

2. Tim is doing a science experiment. He must balance the scale. What is the missing weight?

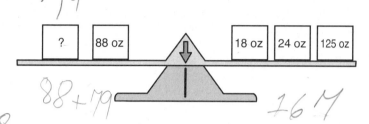

(handwritten: 79)

| ? | 88 oz | 18 oz | 24 oz | 125 oz |

(handwritten: 88 + 79, 167, 88 +79)

How to Do It

Work Backward

A scale is balanced if the total weight on both sides is equal. Work backward to find the missing weight on the left side of the scale.

Find the total weight on the right side of the scale.

18 oz + 24 oz + 125 oz = 167 oz

Find the total weight on the left side of the scale.   88 oz + ? = 167 oz

The total weight on the left side must equal 167 oz to balance the scale.

Use subtraction to find out how many more ounces are needed to balance the scale:

167 oz − 88 oz = 79 oz

The missing weight is 79 oz.

On Your Own

Kelly and Bryan went shopping at the market. They each want to carry the same amount of weight. Which two bags should they each select?

(handwritten: A C / B D)

| 16 lb | 15 lb | 21 lb | 22 lb |
| A | B | C | D |

New Jersey Mathematics Standards
2. **Patterns and Algebra 4.3 D2** Understand and use the concepts of equals, less than, and greater than to describe relations between numbers.

3. **Write a rule for this number pattern and find the next three numbers.**

1, 6, 4, 9, 7, 12, 10, . . .   15 13 18

How to Do It

Find a Pattern

Look for a pattern. Compare the numbers in the pattern.

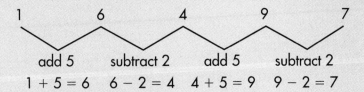

1		6		4		9		7

add 5   subtract 2   add 5   subtract 2
1 + 5 = 6   6 − 2 = 4   4 + 5 = 9   9 − 2 = 7

The pattern is: add 5, subtract 2.

Write a rule for the pattern:

1. Start with 1.

2. Add 5 to the first number to find the second number.

3. Subtract 2 from the second number to find the third number.

4. Continue this pattern of adding 5 and subtracting 2.

Write the next three numbers in the sequence.

1, 6, 4, 9, 7, 12, 10, . . .

Add 5   Subtract 2   Add 5
10 + 5 = 15   15 − 2 = 13   13 + 5 = 18

1, 6, 4, 9, 7, 12, 10, 15, 13, 18

On Your Own

Look at the pattern. Find the missing numbers.

2, 5, 8, ▢, 14, ▢, 20, . . .

This page may not be reproduced without permission of Harcourt Achieve.

New Jersey Mathematics Standards
3. **Patterns and Algebra 4.3 A1** Recognize, describe, extend, and create patterns.

NJ ASK Modeled Instruction ■ 67

4. Eva is saving for a new notebook. She decides to increase her savings each week. Her total savings for the first week was 50¢. The second week, her savings totaled 65¢. Her total savings for week three was 95¢, and week four's total was $1.40. The notebook costs $3.65. How many weeks will it take her to save enough money for the notebook?

How to Do It

Make a Chart, Graph, or List

List the total savings for each week, and find the amount of increase.

Week	Total Savings	Amount of Increase
1	50¢	
		15¢
2	65¢	
		30¢
3	95¢	
		45¢
4	$1.40	
		60¢
5	$2.00	
		75¢
6	$2.75	
		90¢
7	$3.65	

It will take Eva 7 weeks to save enough money for the notebook.

On Your Own

Vince is on the swim team. Each week, he increases the number of laps he swims. How many laps will he swim in week 5?

Week	1	2	3	4	5
Laps	10	14	18	22	26

New Jersey Mathematics Standards
4. **Patterns and Algebra 4.3 A1** Recognize, describe, extend, and create patterns.

SAMPLE PROBLEM

5. Ling is helping her dad tile the square bathroom floor. They are making a pattern like a checkerboard. How many more tiles will they need to finish the pattern?

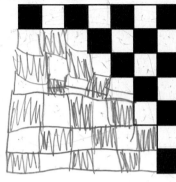

$M \times M = 49$

-20

29

49
29
20

How to Do It

Make a Simpler Problem

You can continue the pattern and count the number of black and white tiles needed to complete the pattern, or you can solve a simpler problem.

Count the number of tiles along the top: 7

Count the number of tiles along the side: 7

Multiply the tiles along the top by the tiles along the side: $7 \times 7 = 49$

Count the number of tiles Ling and her dad have put on the floor so far: 20

Find the number of tiles they need to finish the pattern: $49 - 20 = 29$

They need 29 more tiles to finish the pattern.

On Your Own

How many black tiles and how many white tiles will be on the floor when Ling and her dad finish the pattern?

14 black   25

15 white   24

New Jersey Mathematics Standards
5. Patterns and Algebra 4.3 A1 Recognize, describe, extend, and create patterns.

NJ ASK Modeled Instruction ■ 69

6. Janet had 24 tickets to use at the state fair. She drove the bumper cars, rode the roller coaster, and had a soda and 2 hot dogs. How many tickets does she have left?

3

State Fair	
Food/Ride	Tickets
Bumper Cars	5
Roller Coaster	6
Hot Dog	4
Hamburger	5
Soda	2

-21

How to Do It

Make a Chart, Graph, or List

Find the total number of tickets Janet used on rides, drinks, and food.

Food/Ride	Tickets	Number of Times	Total
Bumper Cars	5	1	5 × 1 = 5
Roller Coaster	6	1	6 × 1 = 6
Soda	2	1	2 × 1 = 2
Hot Dog	4	2	4 × 2 = 8

Total Tickets: 21

24 − 21 = 3 tickets left

Janet had 24 tickets, and she used 21 of them. She has 3 tickets left.

On Your Own

You have 20 tickets to use at Janet's state fair. List one way you can use all the tickets.

20

bumper Cars 1
Roller Coaster 1
Soda 3
Hot dog 3

New Jersey Mathematics Standards
6. **Patterns and Algebra 4.3 C2** Construct and solve simple open sentences involving addition or subtraction (e.g., 3 + 6 = __, n = 15 − 3, 3 + __ = 3, 16 − c = 7).

SAMPLE PROBLEM

7. What picture pattern below follows this letter pattern?

A B A C A B A C

How to Do It

Use Logical Thinking

To write a picture pattern, use a different item for each letter.

The three letters in the letter pattern are A, B, and C. There are three different animal pictures. Let one letter equal one animal:

A = horse   B = dog   C = fox

The answer is B.

A	B	A	C	A	B	A	C
horse	dog	horse	fox	horse	dog	horse	fox

On Your Own

Write a number pattern for the following picture pattern.

AABAACA

New Jersey Mathematics Standards
7. **Patterns and Algebra 4.3 A1** Recognize, describe, extend, and create patterns.

1. **Which number sentence is true?**

   Ⓐ $11 \times 1 = 1$

   Ⓑ $11 + 1 = 11 - 1$

   Ⓒ $11 \div 1 = 1$

   Ⓓ $11 \times 0 = 0 \times 1$

   > ⊚ **Tip:** If the numbers on both sides of the equal sign represent the same amount, the number sentence is true. For each number sentence, use the operation shown to find the value on both sides of the equation. Choose the number sentence where the values are equal.

2. **If this pattern continues, what is the next number?**

   5, 12, 19, 26, ___

   Ⓐ 47

   Ⓑ 40

   Ⓒ 33

   Ⓓ 30

   > ⊚ **Tip:** The numbers in the pattern become greater. Addition and multiplication make numbers greater. Try addition first. Start with the first two numbers. Find what number plus 5 equals 12.

New Jersey Mathematics Standards
1. **Patterns and Algebra 4.3 D1** Understand and apply the properties of operations and numbers.
2. **Patterns and Algebra 4.3 A1** Recognize, describe, extend, and create patterns.

3. **What rule is used to change the input numbers to the output numbers?**

Input	Output
2	4
6	8
10	12
14	16

Ⓐ **add 2**

Ⓑ **subtract 2**

Ⓒ **multiply by 2**

Ⓓ **divide by 1**

🌀 **Tip:** The output numbers are greater than the input numbers. Addition and multiplication make numbers greater. Look at the first set of input and output numbers. You can add: 2 + 2 = 4. Now try multiplication: 2 × 2 = 4. Test your choice on *all* the numbers. The rule must work for every pair of numbers.

New Jersey Mathematics Standards
3. **Patterns and Algebra 4.3 B1** Use concrete and pictorial models to explore the basic concept of a function.

4. **What number makes the number sentence below true?**

$$7 \times \underline{\quad} = 7$$

Ⓐ 7

Ⓑ 1

Ⓒ $\dfrac{1}{7}$

Ⓓ 0

> **🌀 Tip:** Find the missing factor. Remember, when 1 is a factor, the product is the same as the other factor.

5. **What number makes the number sentence below true?**

$$6 + \underline{\quad} = 15$$

Ⓐ 11

Ⓑ 9

Ⓒ 7

Ⓓ 5

> **🌀 Tip:** To find what number added to 6 equals 15, use subtraction.

New Jersey Mathematics Standards
4. **Patterns and Algebra 4.3 D1** Understand and apply the properties of operations and numbers.
5. **Patterns and Algebra 4.3 C2** Construct and solve simple open sentences involving addition or subtraction (e.g., $3 + 6 = \underline{\quad}$, $n = 15 - 3$, $3 + \underline{\quad} = 3$, $16 - c = 7$).

PRACTICE PROBLEMS

6. The graph below shows the average temperature for five months.

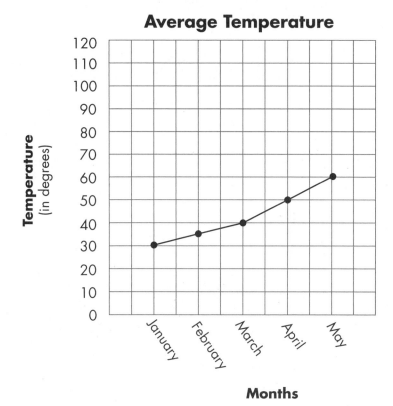

Average Temperature

Which sentence describes how the temperature changes from January to May?

Ⓐ   The temperature stays the same.

Ⓑ   The temperature becomes hotter.

Ⓒ   The temperature becomes cooler.

Ⓓ   There is no pattern to the temperature change.

> ☺ **Tip:** The scale on the left side of the graph shows the temperature in degrees. Find the temperature for each point on the graph. Decide how the temperature changes.

New Jersey Mathematics Standards
6. Patterns and Algebra 4.3 C1 Recognize and describe change in quantities.

NJ ASK Modeled Instruction
Data Analysis, Probability, and Discrete Mathematics

1. Jonathan goes to the park. He sees the items below. He wants to count the number of items he sees and list them in order from fewest to most.

How to Do It

Make a Chart, Graph, or List

Jonathan can make a tally chart to organize the information. It will help him count how many times an item appears. He can use a tally mark "|" to count each item.

Fewest to most: butterflies, caterpillars, beetles, ants, leaves.

Items	Tallies	Total
leaves	ЍЍ II	7
ants	ЍЍ I	6
beetles	ЍЍ	5
caterpillars	IIII	4
butterflies	III	3

On Your Own

How many items did Jonathan see in all? Write 3 other questions for this tally chart.

25

New Jersey Mathematics Standards
1. **Data Analysis, Probability, and Discrete Mathematics 4.4 A2** Read, interpret, construct, analyze, generate questions about, and draw inferences from displays of data.

SAMPLE PROBLEM

2. **This picture shows how a mother duck communicates with her ducklings. List one way she can communicate with duckling 8.**

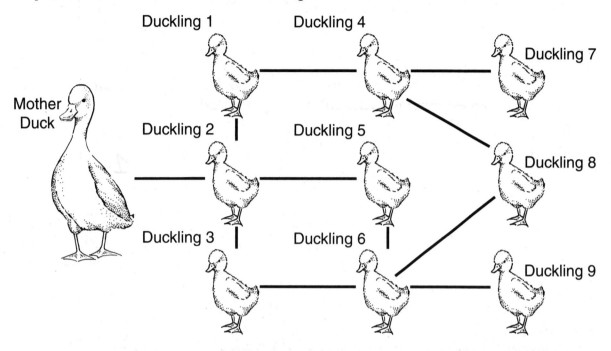

How to Do It

> **Use Logical Thinking**

Find a path from the mother duck to duckling 8. Use "⟶" to show the path.

Duck ⟶ Duckling 2 ⟶ Duckling 1 ⟶ Duckling 4 ⟶ Duckling 8

On Your Own

List two ways Beth can communicate with Jim.

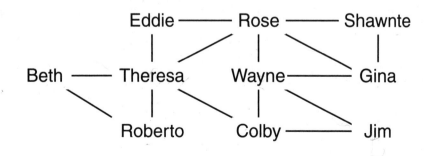

New Jersey Mathematics Standards
2. **Data Analysis, Probability, and Discrete Mathematics 4.4 D2** Explore vertex-edge graphs.

3. Lena spun a spinner 40 times and made a bar graph of her results. Which spinner goes with the graph below?

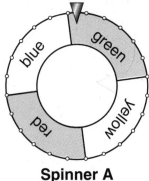

Spinner A

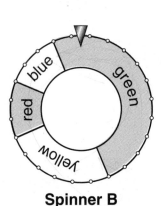

Spinner B

How to Do It

Use Logical Thinking

Look at each spinner and find the chance of getting each of the colors.

Spinner A: The chance of getting any one of the colors is 1 out of 4.

Lena spun the spinner 40 times.

Divide 40 by 4.

The spinner would probably land on any one of the colors 10 times.

Spinner A goes with the bar graph.

On Your Own

Draw a bar graph for Spinner B. Use a separate sheet of paper.

New Jersey Mathematics Standards
3. **Data Analysis, Probability, and Discrete Mathematics 4.4 B1** Use everyday events and chance devices, such as dice, coins, and unevenly divided spinners, to explore concepts of probability and **4.4 A1** Collect, generate, organize, and display data in response to questions, claims, or curiosity.

SAMPLE PROBLEM

4. Pedro decided to list the number of cloudy days for 5 months. This is the table he made. He wants to make a line graph to guess how many cloudy days there will be in August.

Cloudy Days from March to July				
March	April	May	June	July
23	19	15	11	7

How to Do It

Make a Chart, Graph, or List

A line graph is one way to show information and make guesses. Place the months along the horizontal line and the number of days along the vertical line. Plot the points and extend the line to guess the number of cloudy days in August.

Pedro can guess that there might be 3 cloudy days in August.

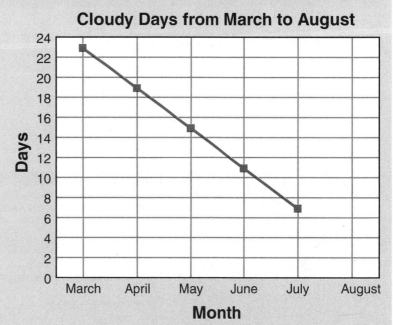

On Your Own

Make a line graph to show the number of cloudy days from September to January.

Cloudy Days from September to January				
September	October	November	December	January
6	12	18	24	27

New Jersey Mathematics Standards
4. **Data Analysis, Probability, and Discrete Mathematics 4.4 A2** Read, interpret, construct, analyze, generate questions about, and draw inferences from displays of data.

5. Marie's class made a pictograph. The graph shows different color jackets owned by third-grade students. How many more blue jackets are there than black jackets?

Third-Graders' Jackets

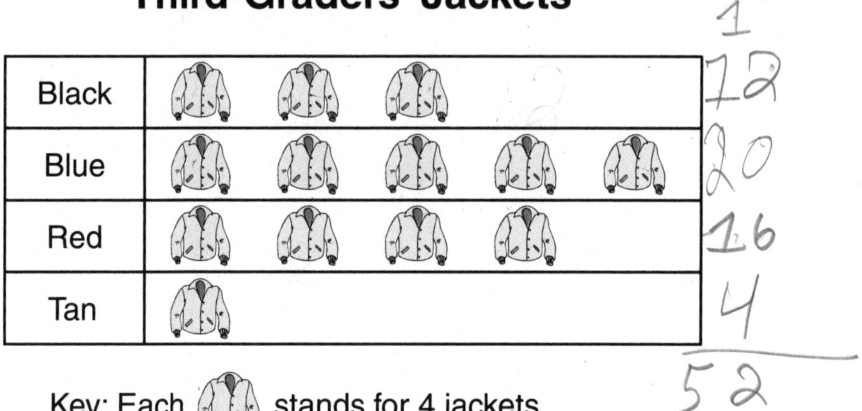

Black	👕 👕 👕
Blue	👕 👕 👕 👕 👕
Red	👕 👕 👕 👕
Tan	👕

Key: Each 👕 stands for 4 jackets.

(handwritten:)
1
12
20
16
4
—
52

8 more

How to Do It — Sort the Data

The key tells you how many jackets each picture stands for.
Find the number of blue and black jackets.

Blue jackets	5×4	=	20
Black jackets	3×4	=	− 12
Find the difference			8

There are 8 more blue jackets than black jackets.

On Your Own

How many jackets are there in all? Which color jacket is the least favorite among the third-grade students?

(handwritten:) Tan   52

New Jersey Mathematics Standards
5. **Data Analysis, Probability, and Discrete Mathematics 4.4 A2** Read, interpret, construct, analyze, generate questions about, and draw inferences from displays of data.

SAMPLE PROBLEM

6. This bag has gum balls of four different colors—red, blue, yellow, and purple. What are your chances of picking a yellow gum ball?

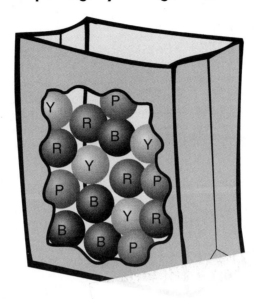

How to Do It

Sort the Da

A *chance* is the possibility of some

picking a yellow gum ball, count t

count the total number of gum ba

Yellow Gum Balls: 4   To

The chances of picking a yello

On Your Own

The letters in the word MULTIPLICATION were put into a hat and picked out one at a time. Which statement is true?

(A) There is a greater chance of picking an "L" than an "I."

(B) There is the same chance of picking an "L" as picking a "T."

(C) There is a lesser chance of picking an "I" than a "T."

(D) There is a greater chance of picking a "P" than an "I."

New Jersey Mathematics Standards

6. **Data Analysis, Probability, and Discrete Mathematics 4.4 B2** Predict probabilities in a variety of situations (e.g., given the number of items of each color in a bag, what is the probability that an item picked will have a particular color).

7. **Bart and his mom are taking a trip to the Fun Facts Museum. His mom wants to take the shortest route. What is the shortest distance to the museum, and through which towns would they travel?**

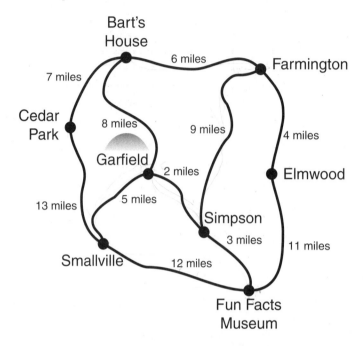

How to Do It

Write a Number Sentence

You can write a number sentence to find the distance from Bart's house to Fun Facts Museum.

Bart's house to Farmington to Simpson to Fun Facts Museum

Distance = 6 + 9 + 3 = 18 miles

Bart's house to Garfield to Simpson to Fun Facts Museum

Distance = 8 + 2 + 3 = 13 miles

Check all other paths. The shortest distance is 13 miles.

On Your Own

Find the longest distance in miles between Bart's house and Fun Facts Museum.

New Jersey Mathematics Standards

7. **Data Analysis, Probability, and Discrete Mathematics 4.4 D1** Follow, devise, and describe practical sets of directions (e.g., to add two 2-digit numbers).

PRACTICE PROBLEM

1. Brenda is at a restaurant. She orders a plate with one meat and two vegetables. She must choose from 2 meats and 3 vegetables. She made the table below to show the different dinners she can make.

Meat	Vegetables		
Chicken	French Fries	Corn	Green Beans
Roast Beef	French Fries	Corn	Green Beans

How many different dinners of 1 meat and 2 vegetables can Brenda make?

Ⓐ 6

Ⓑ 5

Ⓒ 4

Ⓓ 3

🌀 **Tip:** Count the number of dinners Brenda can make with chicken and 2 vegetables. Then count the number of dinners Brenda can make with roast beef and 2 vegetables. Add the two numbers to find the total number of different dinners she can make.

New Jersey Mathematics Standards
1. **Data Analysis, Probability, and Discrete Mathematics 4.4 C2** Represent all possibilities for a simple counting situation in an organized way and draw conclusions from this representation.

2. Jamal needs to color the map. What is the fewest number of colors he can use so that no areas that are the same color touch?

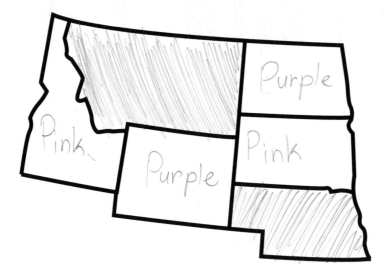

Ⓐ 3

Ⓑ 4

Ⓒ 5

Ⓓ 6

🌀 **Tip:** Find two areas that do not touch. Label them 1. Find an area that touches a 1 and label it 2. Continue to use 2 to label any area that does not touch another 2. When you cannot label any more areas 2, start using the number 3. Continue in the same way. Use as many numbers as you need. Remember, the same two numbers cannot touch each other.

New Jersey Mathematics Standards
2. **Data Analysis, Probability, and Discrete Mathematics 4.4 D3** Find the smallest number of colors needed to color a map.

PRACTICE PROBLEM

3. Calvin made a bar graph to show the number of cars he saw pass his house between 6:00 and 8:30.

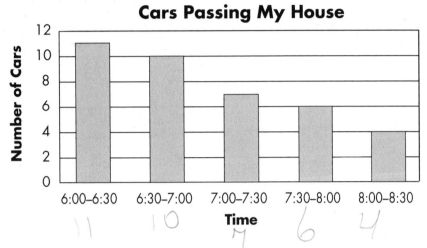

During which time period did Calvin see 7 cars?

   Ⓐ   **6:00–6:30**

   Ⓑ   **6:30–7:00**

   Ⓒ   **7:00–7:30**

   Ⓓ   **7:30–8:00**

> ✆ **Tip:** Look at the scale on the left side of the graph, Number of Cars. The number 7 is between 6 and 8 on the scale. Find the bar that is 7 units tall. Then read the label at the bottom of this bar. The label is the time period when Calvin saw 7 cars.

New Jersey Mathematics Standards
3. **Data Analysis, Probability, and Discrete Mathematics 4.4 A2** Read, interpret, construct, analyze, generate questions about, and draw inferences from displays of data.

4. The Venn diagram shows the number of students in the art club and the number of students in the music club. Each × stands for 1 student.

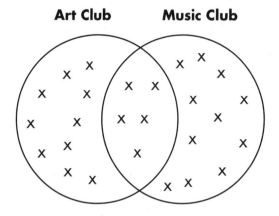

How many students belong to both clubs?

Ⓐ 16

Ⓑ 15

Ⓒ 10

Ⓓ 5

🌀 **Tip:** The two circles overlap. The x's in the overlap go with both circles. They represent students who belong to both clubs.

New Jersey Mathematics Standards
4. **Data Analysis, Probability, and Discrete Mathematics 4.4 C1** Represent and classify data according to attributes, such as shape or color, and relationships.

PRACTICE PROBLEM

DIRECTIONS: The following questions are open-ended questions. Write your answer and show your work in the space following each problem. You may use your calculator.

5. Michael asks students in his class to vote for their favorite fruit. The list below shows the results.

   orange   apple   banana   apple   banana
   apple   banana   apple   apple   plum

   • Use the information above to fill in the chart.

Favorite Fruit

Fruit	Votes
Orange	1
Apple	5
Banana	3
Plum	1

Michael is having a party. He will serve some fruit. Most of the people he invites to the party are in his class at school. What fruit will most likely be the favorite at Michael's party? Explain your answer. *Apple because apple has a chance of $\frac{5}{10}$ thats more than any fruits.*

🌀 **Tip:** Most of the people who will be at Michael's party are also in his class at school. This fact will help you predict the favorite fruit at Michael's party.

New Jersey Mathematics Standards
5. **Data Analysis, Probability, and Discrete Mathematics 4.4 B2** Predict probabilities in a variety of situations (e.g., given the number of items of each color in a bag, what is the probability that an item picked will have a particular color).

6. Draw lines on the circle below to make a spinner. Make the spinner so it follows these rules. Read the rules carefully.

- The spinner has 4 equal parts.

- Each part is labeled red, blue, or green.

- The spinner is most likely to land on a part labeled red.

- The spinner is equally likely to land on a part labeled blue or green.

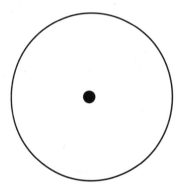

- Complete each statement below.

The probability that the spinner will land on red is _____ out of _____.

The probability that the spinner will land on blue is _____ out of _____.

The probability that the spinner will land on green is _____ out of _____.

⊙ **Tip:** The spinner is most likely to land on the color that appears the greatest number of times. There are 4 equal parts to the spinner. So there are a total of 4 possible places for it to land. To find the probability of spinning each color, count the number of sections with that color. Use this number to fill in the first blank in each sentence above. Use the total number of sections to fill in the second blank.

New Jersey Mathematics Standards
6. **Data Analysis, Probability, and Discrete Mathematics 4.4 B1** Use everyday events and chance devices, such as dice, coins, and unevenly divided spinners, to explore concepts of probability and **4.4 B2** Predict probabilities in a variety of situations (e.g., given the number of items of each color in a bag, what is the probability that an item picked will have a particular color).

NJ ASK Test-Taking Tips

Now you are ready to take the Practice Test for the NJ ASK in Mathematics. Use what you learned in the first section of this book to help you succeed on this practice test.

Use the following tips as you take the Practice Test:

- Read and follow the directions carefully. Ask your teacher to explain anything you do not understand.

- Read each question and ALL the answer choices carefully. Study any pictures, diagrams, and charts.

- Use your Cut-Out Tools when they are needed to answer questions.

- Work out the answer to each problem. If you don't know the answer right away, cross out the answer choices that you know are wrong. Take your best guess from the ones that remain.

- Do not spend too much time on any one question. Skip difficult questions and go back to them later if there is time. Mark items to return to in case there is time.

- For multiple-choice questions, choose the best answer. Fill in the circle next to the answer choice completely. If you want to change your answer, be sure to erase your first answer completely.

- Use any time remaining to check your answers.

- You **may** use a calculator in Sections 2 and 3 of the Practice Test.

Use the following tips for open-ended questions:

- Plan what to write before you begin writing.

- Write your answer neatly in the space provided.

- Some questions have more than one part. Be sure to answer all parts of the question.

- Show all of your work. Answer each question completely.

Name: _____

NJ ASK

GRADE 3 PRACTICE TEST

Mathematics

Directions to the Student

As you are taking this test, remember these important things:

1. Read each question carefully. Choose the correct answer.

2. If you do not know the answer to a question, move on to the next question. You may return to the skipped question later if you have time.

3. When you come to a STOP sign, do **not** turn the page until you are told to do so.

TURN TO THE NEXT PAGE. ➡

DIRECTIONS:

The first section of this test contains 6 multiple-choice questions. You will fill in the circle next to your answer choice. You may NOT use a calculator.

Sample Multiple-Choice Questions

The sample questions below show you what the questions are like and how to mark your answer.

For example:

1. **There are 5 bags and 2 apples are in each bag. What is the total number of apples in all 5 bags?**

    Ⓐ **7**

    ● **10**

    Ⓒ **12**

    Ⓓ **18**

The correct answer is B. The circle with the B in it has been filled in to show that B is the correct answer.

2. **Find the exact value of 5 × 12.**

    Ⓐ **24**

    Ⓑ **52**

    ● **60**

    Ⓓ **70**

The correct answer is C. The circle with the C in it has been filled in to show that C is the correct answer.

GO ON TO THE NEXT PAGE. ➡

DIRECTIONS:

Choose the correct answer for each problem. Fill in the circle next to your answer choice. You may NOT use a calculator.

1. **Find the exact value of 62 × 4.**

   Ⓐ **315**

   Ⓑ **248**

   Ⓒ **108**

   Ⓓ **66**

2. **Estimate 636 − 278. The difference is between which numbers?**

   Ⓐ **0 and 199**

   Ⓑ **200 and 399**

   Ⓒ **400 and 599**

   Ⓓ **600 and 799**

TURN TO THE NEXT PAGE. ➡

3. **Find the exact value of 362 − 281.**

- Ⓐ 79
- Ⓑ 81
- Ⓒ 171
- Ⓓ 643

4. **Find the exact value of 18 + 24 + 157.**

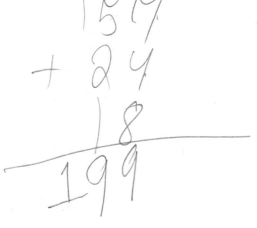

- Ⓐ 209
- Ⓑ 199
- Ⓒ 181
- Ⓓ 175

GO ON TO THE NEXT PAGE. ➡

5. **Find the exact value of 17 × 8.**

- Ⓐ 95
- Ⓑ 135
- Ⓒ 136
- Ⓓ 153

6. **Find the exact value of 285 + 247.**

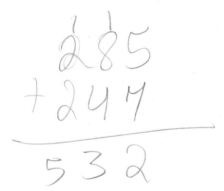

- Ⓐ 532
- Ⓑ 522
- Ⓒ 422
- Ⓓ 397

STOP

If you have time, you may review your work in this section only.

DIRECTIONS:

Choose the correct answer for each problem. Fill in the circle next to your answer choice. You may use your calculator, ruler, or shapes.

7. Which number is closest to 323 on the number line below?

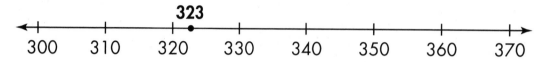

323

300 310 320 330 340 350 360 370

Ⓐ **310**

Ⓑ **320**

Ⓒ **330**

Ⓓ **340**

8. The Venn diagram shows what kinds of music Paul and Amanda like. What kinds of music do they both like?

Paul   Amanda

classical   jazz   rap
country   hip-hop   rock

Ⓐ **classical and jazz**

Ⓑ **jazz and hip-hop**

Ⓒ **hip-hop and rock**

Ⓓ **rap and hip-hop**

GO ON TO THE NEXT PAGE. ➡

9. **A.J. has the six-sided figure shown below. He starts to place a border of squares and triangles around it.**

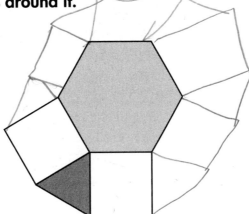

What is the total number of squares and triangles he will need for the border?

Ⓐ   **4 squares, 4 triangles**

Ⓑ   **6 squares, 3 triangles**

Ⓒ   **6 squares, 6 triangles**

Ⓓ   **8 squares, 4 triangles**

10. Look at each pair of numbers. In which pair are both numbers even?

Ⓐ 44, 79

Ⓑ 17, 58

Ⓒ 23, 31

Ⓓ 12, 64

11. On which figure below is it possible to draw a line of symmetry?

Ⓐ

Ⓑ

Ⓒ

Ⓓ

GO ON TO THE NEXT PAGE. ➡

12. Tyra started putting money in her piggy bank. She had saved $6 after the first week. Over the next 4 weeks, she put in the same amount of money each week. The table below shows Tyra's savings.

Amount in Piggy Bank						
Week Number	1	2	3	4	5	6
Total Amount	$6	$12	$18	$24	$30	$36

If Tyra continues to save the same amount each week, how much will she have in her piggy bank after week 6?

Ⓐ $33

Ⓑ $35

Ⓒ $36

Ⓓ $42

13. Which number sentence below is true?

Ⓐ 38 < 19

Ⓑ 40 < 67

Ⓒ 23 > 25

Ⓓ 24 > 52

TURN TO THE NEXT PAGE. ➡

14. About the same number of people visit the museum each day. On Tuesday, 270 people visited the museum. Which is the best estimate of the total number of people who will visit the museum in 4 days?

   Ⓐ   200

   Ⓑ   500

   Ⓒ   800

   Ⓓ   1,200

(handwritten: 270 × 4 = 1080)

15. The small carton holds 2 cups. About how many cups does the large carton hold?

2 cups

   Ⓐ   8 cups

   Ⓑ   4 cups

   Ⓒ   2 cups

   Ⓓ   1 cup

GO ON TO THE NEXT PAGE. ➡

16. The students in Mr. Peterson's class voted for their favorite school subjects. The picture graph shows the results of the vote.

Favorite Subjects

Reading	☺ ☺
Math	☺ ☺ ☺ ☺
Science	☺ ☺ ☺ ☺ ☺ ☺
Social Studies	☺ ☺ ☺

Each ☺ stands for 2 votes.

How many students chose math as their favorite subject?

Ⓐ   **4**

Ⓑ   **6**

Ⓒ   **8**

Ⓓ   **10**

TURN TO THE NEXT PAGE. ➡

17. Which of the figures below has 0 vertices?

Ⓐ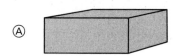

Ⓑ

Ⓒ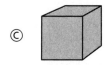

Ⓓ

18. This figure has been covered with tiles. If each tile measures 1 square inch, what is the area of the figure?

Ⓐ   14 square inches

Ⓑ   16 square inches

Ⓒ   18 square inches

Ⓓ   20 square inches

GO ON TO THE NEXT PAGE. ➡

19. Diego wants to use his foot to measure the length of a table. He knows that the length of his foot is 7 inches.

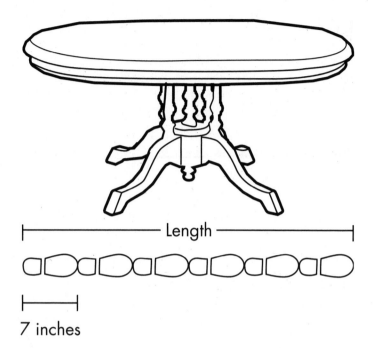

Length

7 inches

What is the length of the table?

Ⓐ   **7 inches**

Ⓑ   **14 inches**

Ⓒ   **28 inches**

Ⓓ   **42 inches**

TURN TO THE NEXT PAGE. ➡

20. Ramon sorted some buttons into two groups, as shown below.

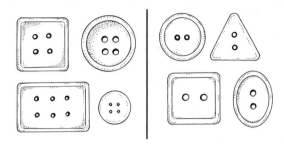

Which sentence describes the rule he used to sort the buttons?

Ⓐ All buttons with more than two holes go in one group.

Ⓑ All buttons with corners go in one group.

Ⓒ All circle-shaped buttons go in one group.

Ⓓ All square buttons go in one group.

21. Which model shows a line?

Ⓐ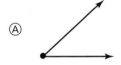

Ⓑ ●————————●

Ⓒ ←————————→

Ⓓ

22. Use your cut-out shapes. Which three shapes can you use to make the figure below?

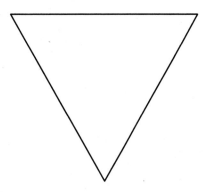

Ⓐ **3 blue rhombuses**

Ⓑ **1 green triangle and 1 blue rhombus**

Ⓒ **2 green triangles and 1 blue rhombus**

Ⓓ **3 green triangles**

If you have time, you may review your work in this section only.

STOP

Directions for Open-Ended Questions

The following questions are open-ended questions. Be sure to:

- Read each question carefully and write the correct answer.
- Answer all parts of each question.
- Show your work and explain your answer.

Questions can be answered using words, tables, diagrams, or pictures. You may use your calculator, ruler, or shapes as needed.

23. Use your ruler to measure each side of the rectangle below in inches.

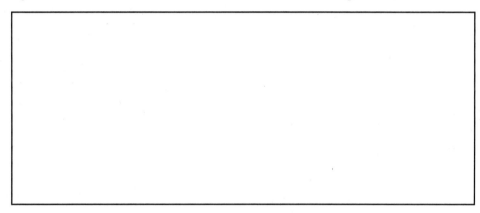

- **What is the perimeter of the rectangle?** 14

Use the grid below to draw the rectangle above. Let each square on the grid stand for 1 square inch.

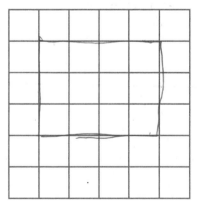

- **What is the area of the rectangle?** 12

GO ON TO THE NEXT PAGE.

24. Look at this number pattern.

43, 37, 31, 25, 19, 13

- Write a rule for finding the next number in the pattern. Explain how to find the rule.

-6 because 37-31=6 and you can keep on doing it and I knew it somehow!

- What are the next three numbers in the pattern? Show your work.

13, 27, 21

25. The students voted on where they should go for their field trip. The votes are shown below.

Activity	Number of Votes
Zoo	7
Baseball Game	11
Museum	4
Movie	8

Use the grid below to make a bar graph that shows the number of students who voted for each place. Include the following on your graph:

• a title

• numbers along the left side to show the scale

• a label for each bar

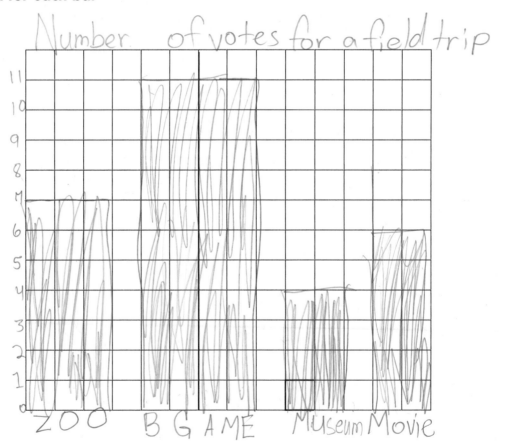

If you have time, you may review your work in this section only.